Basic Care of
Uromastyx

Philippe de Vosjoli

Published by
Advanced Vivarium Systems, Inc.
P.O. Box 6050
Mission Viejo, CA 92690
www.avsbooks.com
(877) 4-AVS-BOOK

Cover photo by David Northcott
Cover design by David Shultz
Printed and Bound in Singapore

Contents

Introduction

The author and his research partner Bob Mailloux have kept uromastyx, also known as spiny-tailed agamids, on and off for the past twelve years. These delightful lizards have become increasingly available out of Egypt in recent years. Unfortunately, the mortality of these imported uromastyx in captivity has been unusually high. Indeed, most imported specimens are dead by the end of their first year in captivity. The cause of death is primarily lack of knowledge about how to establish and maintain these lizards.

Uromastyx have many of the characteristics that make a lizard desirable as a reptile pet: (1) they have an unusual and, in some species, attractive appearance; (2) the two species now imported in large numbers, the Egyptian and the ornate uromastyx, are relatively docile and, with time, develop responsive personalities; (3) once established, these lizards are actually rather easy to care for. An important consideration with the large Egyptian uromastyx (imported in the greatest numbers) is the size of the enclosure required for proper housing. These lizards grow large and eventually require a custom enclosure that occupies a significant portion of a room.

This book was written primarily out of concern for the welfare of the increasing numbers of uromastyx now being imported into the United States. It is not intended to be a comprehensive book on the genus *Uromastyx*, but rather a book that focuses on the basic care of commonly imported species. These are such wonderful animals that every effort should be made to acclimate them to captivity, to maintain them in a responsible manner, and to captive breed them before they are no longer available.

General Information

Common Names
Uromastyx; spiny-tailed agamids; Dab lizards

Taxonomy
Uromastyx were once placed in the family Agamidae, but more recently in the subfamily Leiolepidinae in the family Chameleonidae (Etheridge and Frost, 1989). The genus *Uromastyx* includes ten to twelve species. The only other genus in the subfamily is *Leiolepis*, to which belong the Southeast Asian butterfly agamas, such as the commonly imported (but notoriously difficult to keep alive) *Leiolepis belliana.*

Species Available in Pet Stores
- Egyptian uromastyx *(Uromastyx aegyptius)*, also sold in pet stores as Egyptian spiny-tailed lizards or Egyptian spiny-tailed agamids. This is the largest and most commonly imported species. Their total length is up to 28 inches (71 cm).

- Ornate uromastyx *(Uromastyx ocellatus ornatus).* Only in the two years prior to the writing of this book has this species been imported in significant numbers. Males rank among the most beautiful of all lizards. Their total length is up to 15 inches (38 cm).

- Ocellated uromastyx *(Uromastyx ocellatus ocellatus).* This species is similar to, but not as colorful as, the ornate uromastyx.

- North African uromastyx *(Uromastyx acanthinurus).* Very rarely imported but occasionally available as captive-bred, this is one of the most colorful uromastyx. It is distributed

This photo illustrates the potential size of Egyptian uromastyx. The smaller specimen will be easier to acclimate than the large male shown here.

from Senegal to Egypt. Most of the imported captive stock originated from Morocco. Their total length is up to 18 inches (45.7 cm).

▪ *Uromastyx benti,* sometimes sold as red uromastyx, are occasionally imported from Yemen. Their total length is up to 15 inches (38 cm).

▪ Hardwick's uromastyx *(Uromastyx hardwicki).* This species was once sporadically imported from Pakistan but is increasingly rare in the pet trade in recent years. Their total length is up to 10 ½ inches (26.7 cm).

Sexing

Egyptian uromastyx males develop pronounced femoral pores, particularly in the spring, when pore secretions form scale-like fringes on the underside of the thighs. The males of Egyptian uromastyx also grow larger than females, are somewhat less heavy-bodied, and have somewhat larger heads. Ornate uromastyx are sexually dimorphic; the males are more brightly colored, have wider heads, grow larger, and in the spring produce a fringe of femoral pore secretions along the thighs. The Moroccan uromastyx may be difficult to sex accurately outside of the breeding season. In the spring, following a cooling period, the males produce significant pore secretions and develop postanal bulges.

Longevity

There is little information on the longevity of uromastyx in captivity, but the available records suggest that these are relatively long-lived lizards. Slavens and Slavens (1992) note the following longevity records for uromastyx: *Uromastyx aegyptius*, 15 years 4 months and 12 years; *Uromastyx acanthinurus*, 11 years 5 months and 9 years 6 months; *Uromastyx ocellatus*, 3 years 9 months. The author has a specimen of *Uromastyx acanthinurus* currently out on breeding loan, which was captive-bred in Europe and is now 12 years old. Improved husbandry methods and captive raising from hatchlings should eventually result in significantly higher captive longevities.

Sociability

Interspecific aggression can be common in all species of *Uromastyx*, but particularly in the spring during the breeding season. It is generally best to keep them in small groups of one male to two or three females. Having multiple groups that can observe each other through glass may help stimulate breeding. With *Uromastyx aegyptius* and *Uromastyx o. ornatus*, specimens raised together tend to form hierarchies that may be compatible in large enclosures. *Uromastyx acanthinurus* males and females are equally aggressive. They can be kept in trios, but gravid females should be monitored. Females of this species may kill members of both sexes.

Status

All species of *Uromastyx* are listed under Appendix II of Convention on International Trade in Endangered Species (CITES). This means that CITES permits are required for their transport between countries. Most species are threatened.

The Egyptian uromastyx and other large species are sold for food in local markets in their countries of origin. In some areas smaller species and specimens are collected for the pet trade.

Recommendations

As a group, uromastyx have great potential as reptile pets; however, if current trends continue, before very long they will no longer be available. It is therefore urgent that herpetoculturists develop the methods for long-term and self-sustaining captive breeding of all uromastyx species. Programs should be implemented in the countries of origins for sound management and ranching of these lizards. The day when uromastyx are no longer available in the reptile trade, we will all look back and wonder how we could have been so short-sighted as to allow such great lizards to slip out of our lives. Heed this warning!

Selection

The species imported in greatest numbers is the Egyptian uromastyx; the following step-by-step approach to selection focuses on this species. You should perform the following detailed examination when selecting imported Egyptian uromastyx:

- Unless you are experienced at establishing this species, avoid large adult animals. They are difficult to acclimate and to establish in captivity. Furthermore, they usually require large, custom-built enclosures. Healthy juveniles and small subadults tend to adapt much more readily to captivity.

- Select an animal that appears robust, active and alert. Avoid thin animals. Many of these show a pronounced outline of the backbone and thin tails.

- Ask that the animal you intend to select be shown to you. The animal should demonstrate signs of muscular vigor and activity. Limp, inactive animals are usually unhealthy. When in hand a healthy uromastyx should give the impression of having some weight relative to its size. Ask to see it's belly or, if the pet store personnel allows you to handle the selected animal, turn it so as to examine it's belly area.

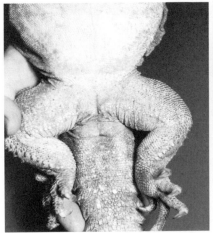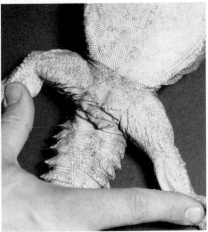

Male (left) uromastyx usually have more pronounced femoral (thigh) pores than females (right). In some species this is more obvious during the breeding season. Note the slightly enlarged postanal bulge in the male and well developed preanal pores in the female.

- Avoid animals that have thin tails. In these animals the tail area to the side of the spine will appear collapsed and thin. The middle area of the tail will appear markedly raised (vertebral outline). In contrast, the tails of potentially healthy animals are rounded without a pronounced raised middle area.

- If the animal has dried smeared feces, visible as large brown spots around the vent area and extending onto the tail area, then the probability is high that the animal has internal parasites, very likely amoebiasis or other protozoans. Avoid such animals.

- Check the animal carefully for surface wounds, broken ribs (sections of the side will appear collapsed), infected toes (swollen), eye or mouth problems, which appear as asymmetries; healthy lizards are bilaterally symmetrical.

Other Species

The general rule regarding selecting younger rather than adult animals applies to other species; however, adults of ornate, ocellated, and North African uromastyx adapt more readily than adult Egyptian uromastyx. You should keep in mind that this is relative, considering that ornate and ocellated uromastyx of any size are generally more difficult to establish than Egyptian uromastyx.

Acclimation

Quarantine

Because imported animals are typically infected with parasites, you should always keep them separate from other uromastyx and reptiles in your collection. At least keep them in a separate enclosure, and preferably in a separate room.

Notes on Acclimation

Standard maintenance procedures should be followed during acclimation, and the following is essential for acclimating imported animals. Beware of claims of captive-bred uromastyx; with the exception of *U. acanthinurus*, these claims are commonly false, although occasionally captive-hatched animals are available.

As soon as possible, have a qualified veterinarian examine a fecal sample for parasites. Many imported uromastyx are infected with amoebas or other protozoans, so you should implement treatment as soon as possible. Many experienced herpetoculturists routinely treat all imports with Panacur® (fenbendazole) and with Flagyl® (metronidazole) with good results. A key sign of gastroenteritis, including amoebiasis, is runny stools, very different than the semifirm pellets of healthy animals. One of the most important protocols for establishing the beautiful ornate uromastyx is the combined treatment of nematode infections and amoebic infections. See the section *Diseases and Disorders* for more information.

> Treatment for parasites is critical for establishing most imported species of uromastyx.

Uromastyx of all sizes are primarily vegetarian.

During the first week of acclimation and during treatment for parasites, rehydrating uromastyx is very important. Place the uromastyx, front body only, in a shallow pan of lukewarm water for five to ten minutes once or twice a day. Disinfect containers with 5% bleach solution between soakings. Rinse before adding clean water. Leaving a water dish in a uromastyx enclosure is not a good idea. The water can become a vector for reinfection by parasites; it can allow the growth of bacteria and will quickly be overturned onto the substrate by these active lizards. Sick animals should also be hydrated through injection. Consult a veterinarian for this procedure.

During the deparasitization stage of acclimation, you should keep uromastyx on newspaper. Once treatment is completed you can shift them to a more suitable substrate such as alfalfa pellets.

Housing and Maintenance

Enclosures

You can keep uromastyx in all-glass vivaria with screen tops, in custom-made wood or melamine-coated wood vivaria, in plastic sided enclosures with screen tops, or in other large box-type enclosures.

Enclosure size

The length of the vivarium should be at least four times the length of the animal and the width at least twice the length of the animal.

Substrate

Use newspaper for substrate during the initial acclimation of your imported animals so that you can monitor the state of the feces. Later you can maintain the animals on alfalfa pellets or medium-grade pea gravel, large enough that ingestion is unlikely. The advantage of pea gravel is that it provides a surface that can help wear down the lizard's nails. When these lizards are kept on alfalfa pellets on newspaper, their nails may grow too long, eventually causing the digits to twist and resulting in problems that may lead to infection.

Play sand, limestone sand, or decomposed granite sand are suitable substrates for adult animals, but hatchlings and juveniles may ingest sand, which can lead to impaction. (The author has had two deaths of hatchling *U. benti* from sand impaction.) Follow instructions on feeding to minimize the risk of substrate ingestion and impaction.

Landscaping the Vivarium

Shelters: Uromastyx are generally burrowers, although some species such as ornate uromastyx are rock dwellers and simply dig subrock shelters, while Egyptian uromastyx are ground dwellers and dig deep burrows. The author has kept *Uromastyx aegyptius* in large outdoor enclosures (16 x 8 ft or 4.9 x 2.4 m) and can attest to their burrowing tendencies. Indoors, provide your uromastyx with shelters of cork bark, wood, rock, or fiberglass. If you use rocks, they should be firmly anchored together with concrete or adhesives, or be heavy enough so that once they are assembled in a shelter-creating pile, there is no risk that an animal will displace a rock by digging and be accidentally crushed. Shelters provide a low-stress environment and protection from light, heat, and intraspecies interaction.

Basking Sites

To create a basking site, place one or more flat rocks directly under a spotlight. The rocks will absorb some of the heat and provide areas for thermoregulation. If you keep more than two or more specimens together, provide an additional basking light because of competition if only a single site is provided.

Rocks: Flattened or large, rounded rocks placed on the surface of the substrate allow for nail wear and are recommended, particularly when alfalfa or newspaper is used as a substrate.

Plants: Uromastyx will destroy most plant material within their reach but will not harm plants that are placed out of their reach. Cylindrical and semicylindrical "snake plants," such as *Sansevieria cylindrica* and *Sansevieria ehrenbergi* will be nibbled initially and possibly scarred, but eventually they will be left alone. Large cow-tongue plants *(Gasteria)* are also suitable, as are ponytail palms with a crown well above ground level. Yuccas will work in outdoor vivaria, as well as similar plants with thick trunks and foliage that is out of reach of ground-dwelling uromastyx. Plants are certainly not required when keeping uromastyx, but if you prefer them in the vivarium, careful selection will allow you to keep some plants with these primarily vegetarian animals.

Heating

Place a subtank heating strip on a rheostat beneath the tank to maintain ambient daytime temperatures in the upper 80s° F (30 to 36.7° C) during the day. At night the temperature should drop to the 70s° F (21.1 to 26.1° C). Placing the subtank heat strip on a timer to allow the temperature to drop to room

Subadult ornate uromastyx on a commercially produced concrete shelter. This rock dwelling species require shelters, and cork bark or rock to create an enriched captive environment.

temperature during the warmer months of the year will work fine. (For winter temperatures, see information on hibernation in *Breeding* section.) In addition you must place a spotlight over a wide basking area so that the temperature of the basking area closest to the bulb measures 100-110° F (37.8 to 43.3° C). The basking spotlight should be on 12 to 14 hours per day and turned off at night. If you keep more than one or two animals together, then you should incorporate more than one spotlight and basking site into the design. Failure to provide enough heat can lead to a number of problems, including gastroenteric disease and metabolic bone disease.

Note: It is critical that at least 50 percent of a vivarium be out of range of the spotlight and basking area so that the animals can thermoregulate (adjust their body temperature by selecting the vivarium location that fits their needs at any given time).

Lighting

For all *Uromastyx* species, the author recommends a four-bulb fluorescent fixture running the length of the enclosure: three full-spectrum bulbs, such as Vita Lite,® or ReptiSun® UVB 310, and one BL-type blacklight. You should place this fluorescent fixture, or two double bulb fixtures, on a timer to run twelve to fourteen hours each day. This lighting is required for keeping *Uromastyx o. ornatus*. Without it and/or natural sunlight, symptoms of metabolic bone disease will develop in this species within six months to two years. (See below).

Sunlight

The author has raised *Uromastyx aegyptius* indoors from hatchlings and has kept them for three years before donating them to the research facilities at White Mountain Junior High School in Rock Springs, Wyoming. The animals to date appear to be of normal size and healthy; in the spring of 1995 they were observed copulating. On the other hand, *Uromastyx o. ornatus* has been a source of problems that developed after 3 months with some imported specimens and after 12 to 24 months with captive-raised animals. These problems have included symptoms of metabolic bone disease, which in *Uromastyx ornatus* shows itself in the form of bumps along the backbone, collapse of the backbone, paralysis of the hindlimbs, complete paralysis and death. This disease occurred in spite of care to provide a proper diet and supplementation.

The causes of the problem are linked to vitamin D_3 and calcium in some way, either to too much D_3 and calcium leading to kidney damage, or problems in absorbing dietary D_3 or calcium deficiency. The best solution would be to expose captive animals to 6 to 12 hours a week of natural sunlight when conditions allow and during that time eliminate or drastically reduce vitamin D_3 from the diet. It is possible that the above mentioned symptoms may be linked to more than one cause. Only further experimintation and research will allow us to get to the root of this syndrome.

Relative Humidity

Uromastyx, as a rule, do not do well if kept at a high relative humidity. These are desert lizards that will fair best at low to moderate relative humidity, up to 65%. In high relative humidity areas, they should be kept indoors with a dehumidifier placed in the room.

Feeding

Hatchling and juvenile uromastyx generally adapt better to captivity and are less discriminating feeders than adults, particularly in the case of larger, adult Egyptian uromastyx. These will definitely tax the limits of your patience and your stress tolerance before they finally adapt to their captive conditions, including diet.

Uromastyx are primarily vegetarian, but some of them also have a propensity for eating insects, depending on the species. Of the species currently available in pet stores, the adult Egyptian uromastyx is the most exclusively vegetarian.

Diet

A working captive diet consists of the following items.

Plant matter: (1) 60 to 75 percent chopped leafy greens, including endive, kale, mustard greens, spinach (small amounts only), collard greens and, when available, mulberry leaves and hibiscus leaves and flowers; (2) 25 to 40 percent thawed frozen vegetables such as peas, green beans, and lima beans; also grated carrots and squashes, (3) once a week, dried split peas and bird seed.

Plant matter feeding schedule: Once daily.

Other foods: Commercial iguana diets are often accepted by younger uromastyx. Until the long-term effects of these diets have been evaluated with uromastyx, however, commercial iguana diets should make up only a portion of a varied diet. There may be problems with some of the iguana diets with these species. For example, some herpetoculturists have noted that with some commercial iguana diets, uromastyx develop crusty mouth edges, resulting from bacterial or possibly fungal growth. Excessive sugar has been hypothesized as the possible cause. If you observe such symptoms in your uromastyx, switching to natural foods or to other iguana diets will usually remedy the situation.

Supplementation: A mixture consisting of three parts reptile vitamin and mineral supplement, such as Herptivite® or

This is a life-size photo of the head of a large Egyptian uromastyx. These lizards are rather intelligent and responsive and should be provided with the right captive conditions and diet.

Reptivite®, combined with one part calcium carbonate plus one part dried edible brewer's yeast (a good B vitamin source, available at health food stores), sprinkled lightly on the plant vegetable mix twice a week for immature animals and once a week for adults.

Insects: Crickets of the appropriate size (length no more than 3/4 the length of the head of the lizard) should be offered 2 to 3 times weekly to immature animals in amounts that will be consumed at one feeding. Adult animals should be offered insects once every 10 to 14 days. Waxworms (the caterpillars of the wax moth *Galleria melonella*) also are relished by uromastyx of all sizes. Adults of most species of uromastyx can be offered mealworms and king mealworms *(Zophobas morio)*. The latter are relished by most species but should be offered only in small amounts (2 to 3 per feeding for *U. aegyptius* and 1 to 2 per feeding for smaller species). With immature animals, you should coat insects with a vitamin-and-mineral-supplement once per week.

❏ Feed plant matter daily.

❏ Supplement plant matter 2 times per week for immature, once a week for adults

❏ Offer insects to lizards twice a week for immature, once every 10-14 days for adults.

❏ Water through light misting or brief soaking once per week.

Water

Because newly imported uromastyx are typically dehydrated, the author recommends light misting of individual animals for one to two minutes once or twice each day for the first two weeks. This will often incite drinking behavior. Misting should be done over a paper substrate that can easily be replaced, *never* over sand or alfalfa pellets. (The sand will cling to the animals' bodies; the alfalfa will swell, become soggy, and eventually begin to decompose.) After this two-week period and the initial deparasitizing, animals can be misted lightly once a week, again not over sand or alfalfa. An alternative is to soak animals once a week in a shallow container of clean, lukewarm water. Disinfect the soaking container with a 5-percent solution of bleach in water. Wash the container with this solution and rinse it thoroughly; do this after each soak to avoid the risk of spreading possible contamination from one animal to another. Uromastyx obtain most of their water from their food, although it is hypothesized that they also obtain water from dew in the wild. Do not keep containers of water in their enclosures as a permanent fixture; this practice can lead to several diseases, including fungal and bacterial infections.

North African uromastyx (Uromastyx acanthinurus). This species has proven to breed readily in captivity and is offered through specialized reptile dealers. Photo by D.B. Travis.

Breeding

Breeding success with uromastyx thus far has been infrequent and sporadic. By far the species most commonly bred in captivity in Europe and in the United States is the North African uromastyx *(Uromastyx acanthinurus)*. In their countries of origin, research on breeding has been successful with animals kept year round in outdoor pens. In all species of uromastyx bred to date, prebreeding conditioning is initiated by reducing the photoperiod to ten hours of daylight per day and gradual cooling. Hibernation or brumation is a requirement for the successful breeding of this species. In California, Robert Mailloux, my research partner, has allowed *Uromastyx acanthinurus* to dig burrows and spend the winters in sheltered screenhouses outdoors; he has had a certain amount of success at captive-breeding.

Several private herpetoculturists and zoos have achieved excellent results with hibernating or cooling their animals indoors. The general procedure for winter cooling is as follows. Starting on December 1, reduce the photoperiod to 8 to 10 hours of daylight, and turn off all heat sources other than a daytime spotlight, thus allowing the background temperature to drop to approximately room temperature. Stop feeding the animals. After two weeks, turn off the spotlight and maintain the animals at an ambient temperature of 57 to 68° F (14 to 20° C). On March 1 reset all heaters and lights to previous maintenance levels and resume normal feeding. Breeding typically will occur in April and egglaying in May or June. The eggs should be placed in a barely damp Perlite® or sand and vermiculite, or in a peat moss and sand mixture. Simple polystyrene foam incubators such as the Hovabator® will work well, as long as they are properly calibrated. Incubation is nearly three months at a temperature of 85 to 90° F (29.4 to 32.2° C).

Diseases and Disorders

Internal Parasites

The two main problems with imported uromastyx are internal parasites (particularly amoebiasis), other protozoans, and round worms. Particularly in *Uromastyx o. ornatus*, the combination of amoebiasis and nematode worms may lead to septicemia, which is fatal, according to Dr. Matthew Moyle, who has considerable experience with uromastyx. He recommends administering oral chloramphenicol in conjunction with the parasite treatments Flagyl® (metronidazole) and Panacur® (fenbendazole). When the author adopted this protocol, success at establishing imported *Uromastyx o. ornatus* increased considerably. An experienced veterinarian should be consulted during this acclimation period for *U. o. ornatus*, particularly if their stools are watery.

Healthy uromastyx have semi-solid, reasonably well-formed stools. If the stools of your animals are liquid or runny, then waste no time in seeking the advice of an experienced reptile veterinarian.

A well designed set-up for Egyptian uromastyx.

Diet-related Problems

Another problem common to uromastyx is respiratory infection. It may be that when these animals are kept in mixed collections, some of the viruses affecting other species have very deleterious effects on uromastyx. Symptoms of respiratory infection include mucus emerging from nostrils, listlessness, and watery eyes that seem half opened. When you notice any of these symptoms, check to be sure that you are keeping your animals at a high enough temperature and at low to moderate relative humidity. If the animals appear weak and are not feeding, immediately consult a qualified veterinarian. These respiratory infections are usually treatable.

Spinal Problems

Uromastyx are not used to encountering a vertical transparent surface (such as a clear glass cage wall) and some individuals will persist in digging at the edge and arching their back in such a way that they collapse the backbone. Seen from above, the back of the lizard will appear collapsed rather than slightly arched, a problem that tends to occur commonly with *Uromastyx o. ornatus*. To prevent this, place rock barriers along the sides of the enclosure, or keep your animals in large landscaped enclosures.

Renal Failure and Gout

Gout characterized by uric-acid deposits in the kidneys and other organs is associated with excessive protein in the diet, excessive dietary D_3, lack of hydration, and renal failure. The herpetoculturist can prevent this fatal disease by paying attention and fulfilling the husbandry and dietary requirements of these animals.

References

Frost, D.R., and R. Etheridge. 1989. A Phylogenetic Analysis and Taxonomy of Iguanian Lizards. Misc. Publ. No. 81, University of Kansas Museum of Natural History.

Grow, D. 1991. "Lizard Management at the Oklahoma City Zoological Park with Special Reference to *Uromastyx, Chamaeleo* and *Heloderma*" in *Proceedings of the 15th International Herpetological Symposium on Captive Propagation and Husbandry*, pp. 161–172.

Slavens, F., and K. Slavens. 1992. *Reptiles and Amphibians in Captivity: Breeding, Longevity and Inventory*. Seattle, Slaveware.

Thatcher, T. 1994. "The Reproduction in Captivity of the North African Spiny-tailed Lizard *(Uromastyx acanthinurus)*" in *Breeding Reptiles and Amphibians*, edited by Simon Townson. British Herpetological Society, Pp. 45–50.

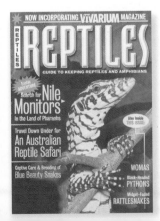